THE BRIGHT PLAIN

THE

BRIGHT PLAIN

by

Charles Edward Eaton

CHAPEL HILL

The University of North Carolina Press

1942

COPYRIGHT, 1942, BY
THE UNIVERSITY OF NORTH CAROLINA PRESS

Acknowledgments are due to the following magazines for permission to reprint poems: *Harper's, The Virginia Quarterly Review, The Yale Review, Poetry: A Magazine of Verse, The American Mercury, The North American Review, Voices, American Prefaces, The Southwest Review, The Lyric, The American Scholar, Fantasy, The Sewanee Review, Furioso, The Washington Post, The University Review* (Kansas City), and *Queen's Quarterly* (Canada).

To

MY MOTHER AND FATHER

Contents

PART I

THE BRIGHT PLAIN

The Bright Plain	15
Spring Song	16
Green Regions	17
High Noon	18
Afternoon in Summer	19
Inlet	20
Stand Here: Near Me	21
Evening Equipoise	22
Tempo of the Night	23
Night Song	25
The Body's Dawn	26
Distant Victory	27

PART II

LANDSCAPE OF THE MIND

Landscape of the Mind	31
Cold Spring	32
The Snake	33
Ask Not of Me	34
Night Quest	35
Voyage	36
The Curtain of Rain	37
Love Song	38

Target Light 39
The Hurt Look of Evil 40
The Tree Stands Tenser 41
The Truce 42
Blind Would Be the Spirit 43
Nocturne 45

PART III

NIGHT TAKES THE CITY

Night Takes the City 49
Lost in Limbo 50
The Hunted 51
The Purchase 52
Declaration of the Snow 53
To Pedestrians of a Foreign Land 54
Other-Faces 55
Night Walk 56
Fountain 57
New Year 58
Street Scene 59
Beer Parlor 60
Equal Pace 61
Affirmation of the Evening 62

PART IV

SUMMIT AIR

Dark Summer 65
Talisman 66

Memory	67
Girls in White	68
Burning Leaves	69
A Ritual in Time of Death	70
The Purest Fact	72
A Play Called Eternity	73
Summit Air	74
These Are the Things of Youth	75
Vernal City	76
Summer Night	77
What Is the Earth Compounded of	78

PART V

DAWN FLIGHT

A Letter to a Young American	83
Air Raid	84
The Land Is Made of Light	85
Matinal	86
The Disparate Man	87
Old House	88
Pivot Place	89
Dawn Flight	90
Sheen of My Sensation	91
Light in Time Only	92

PART I

THE BRIGHT PLAIN

The Bright Plain

This has been a day
    luxurious and lilting and spun
    like a long-linked spool of brightness from the sun.

This has been a day
    like the first stanza: beginning rhyme
    of the song-drift (da capo: da capo) of importunate
                                           time.

This has been a day
    when life-long travelers through the glistening world
    found air lavish: prodigal: the landscape hurled

In glinting rock:
    sun-lake and long legato green.
    Joy was the way breath leaned

Like a fresh wind
    into day, barely ruffling the grass, the landscape's ease,
    leaving desire unhorizoned: the bright plain between
                                            distant trees.

Spring Song

The day is like a bell
Rung suddenly in many tones of green,
Sprung full and clear-toned well
Into the rounded air. . . .
                        I had been
Jarred by all the jagged friction of the world,
The clap-tone in my ear of lashing sound,
When the great swaying swirl of spring was hurled
In thunderous green against the ground. . . .
                                Staccato ring
Time's carillons, purging here-and-now;
Like lurching bells, the new leaves swing
Along the leaping bough.

Green Regions

Epiphanies of green the heart can learn,
Detected by the quick blood's restless compass,
Instruct divergent routes of mind to turn
In true directions. My body stands on grass,
And the thresh of pulse says this is mine.
The shining rock is welded to my hand,
Thought moves magnetic toward the glinting pine;
This is my breath that swells within the land.
The blood is the traveler's only guide,
A richly charted map within his veins;
When stars black out and continents slide,
This is the accurate compass that remains.
So in uncertain lands with a hostile race,
I chart green regions on a barren place.

High Noon

Untarnished yet sun's brilliance holds
The glint-glow mobile on the grass;
Quick light, glissading, still unfolds
Its rippled bars on birds that pass.

Across the landscape's lacquered length
Air's clarity makes distance small.
Beyond the field boys test their strength;
Our listening sight records their fall.

Diminutive is earth where ease
Of day can bring the lake's end near;
No range of land beyond the trees
Can lift topography of fear.

With shadowed farness nowhere seen
And sky bright-stilted on clear light,
We find in mind an inner sheen
To gloss the vistas of the night.

Afternoon in Summer

This suppleness of sun
                this loose girdle of light
That runs glistening and sinuous round the hours of
                              afternoon
Is too complete: a bland repletion where the unignited
Memory of you
              will die the easy death of all that is serene,
Turned in the slow air of vague urge. . . .
                        And soon,
I shall bind up the wilted contemplations of all that you
                              have been
Unless
      these tiger lilies blooming here: riotous: summer's
                            trumpet blast,
      and all the hot rebellion of this pool's sunset
                            reflections
      stir some contending motion in mind's migrant past;
Unless love reclaims the dying,
                linking all early miraculous
                            affections
Past vagary: past oblivion. Prods memory to surprise,
Making time glitter with our backward glance: the furious
                            fervor of our eyes.

Inlet

Away from roiling world
We looked into a bay
Where lurching thought had hurled
The torn and ravaged day.

Wind was in other skies,
The windless landscape spread
Nothingness before our eyes,
Lavish space above our head.

The bell of thought chimed clear
The crystal day's increase,
And all that we could hear
Were syllables of peace.

Secure from bitter verge
Of sea grass and salt wind,
We felt the low waves surge
Through inlet of the mind.

Sea water spent of snare
Unwound its tight-furled din;
The day sailed calmly there
In harbors deep within.

Stand Here: Near Me

Stand here: near me
                where the light of afternoon,
The long-lacquered sheen of persistent gold
Flows like a nimbus round your head. . . .

                              I know that soon
Day will be twilight: the copper-calm: the cold
Ensuing sky of slate: landscape of lead . . .
                      where love is deciduous:
Is ripe for dropping: awaits only the chisel wind of night.

Stand here: near me. . . .
                  I can bear it thus.
The warm insinuations of your lips confound the air,
The murderous certain nisus of our love toward death.
I can bear it longer thus: yet a little longer . . . care.

Evening Equipoise

So in the balanced hour of light
When wind and mind find equipoise,
The pivot-ease of earth turns night
Upon our senses without noise.

As bevel wings of birds drift by,
The lake records smooth duplicates;
A cloud, immobile in the sky,
Is moored by fire till sun abates.

Young boys no longer run up hill
But walk unhurried through the park;
Discrediting the active will,
They seek a tunnel through the dark.

The feud we kept with quick and slow
Must hold the truce the winds declare;
The heart, equilibrate, will know
The flawless peace of equal air.

Tempo of the Night

O deep night when the smell of the earth
Is a scent remembered and all the long stretch
Of the land is a thing remembered,
And the curve of the stallion's neck is blended
With the arching of bridges, the desire
Of the foot to leap wider than rivers,
The wish of the hand to grasp higher than heaven,
The day-long run of the blood, its fearing
And loving—I think the night receives them.
I think the tempo of the night is love
Remembered.

    Today I spoke to the land
With the voice of a lover, matching my words
To the green breadth of grasses. I spoke
To the land with words like clean fingers,
Tangent and mobile, thrust in earth's richness.
I spoke to the earth and almost possessed it,
But the night came . . .

    Today I saw faces
Like all the seasons: beautiful summer,
The leap in the meadow of shining white horses,
And deepest winter, words spoken like cymbals,
The snow caching all sorrow, and the rush
Of the spring like a glittering green fountain.
I saw these swinging landscapes in their eyes,
And almost learned the meaning of the contours.
I felt the changing weather of their faces,
And almost learned which season was the true one,
But the night came . . .

                    Today I heard—
When the wind was silent and the children
Were silent as if time had admonished them
This was the moment—today I heard—
When breath was a tympanum of anguished
Suspension and blood was a tingling like
Death in the throat cords—the word spoken,
The words of the lover, the greening of phrases
As if in the springtime, the ritual
Of lip-touch, solemn and lovely,
The careening of pulse-beat on toward
The evening:
            And night came . . .

                            I think
The tempo of the night is love remembered.

Night Song

I saw the moon unwind
A cloud-coifed skein of light;
The world within my mind
Wore colors of the night.
The trees thatched close with dark
Shadowed the day unspun;
Breath's golden glistening arc
Had spindled like the sun.
The bird whose song was caught
Bright-coiled within his throat
Sang to the stars and sought
The last releasing note.
And hours held in my hand,
Furled glinting in my keep,
Moonwise upon the land
Unwound a skein of sleep.

The Body's Dawn

Tonight clear stars after a long day's rain
Spread a light-ease over the lucid land.
Lustrous flows the river of wind again
In a pure bath of coolness on my hand.
The touch of you is fresh and virginal;
Memory of your lips is time-washed-new.
When we walk to the balanced rise and fall
Of breath, white is the thought that you move through.

In this evening Eden calm with lustral light
There is not a dull star tarnished with time.
Poised on the silent axis of the night,
We stand in the park watching the moon climb:
Waiting immobile on the flawless lawn
Till restive arms unfold the body's dawn.

Distant Victory

Accent of morning
              .   is this sun,
This cascade of light upon the world,
This general brilliance heaven-spun.

Accent of the blood
                   is its unfurled
Silken synergy, smoothly running: calm:
Steady with the liberal memory of joy, the night's deep
                                                         sleep:
The exquisite throbbing pressure of palm to palm:

The intertwined flowing
                     of desire, the pure sweep
Of our need from lip to lip. This breath, this richest sound,
Is the accent of our love: bright cadenza of communion
When day is a lariat of gold upon the ground,

And the accent of time
                      is a tensile glittering bridge:
Bright span out of memory: leaving room ahead:
The unfolding affluence of tranquil days:
Distant victory of things unspoken: yet unsaid.

PART II
LANDSCAPE OF THE MIND

Landscape of the Mind

When I had seen the withering grass,
I wished for crystal in its leaf.
I saw the swan, death-loving, pass,
And watched the pole star of belief

Shift and swing in a golden arc
Till I was sure the earth was turned
In a mad whirl of light and dark
Whose senseless course I had not learned.

So I wished permanence in things,
The emerald leaf blown in the night;
I dressed the birds in armored wings
And tossed the dead rose out of sight.

When I had girded time with stone,
I still smelled chaos in the wind,
Creation burning at my bone,
Shaking the landscape of my mind.

Death was the crystal in my thought
And shaped the contours of my brain;
The emerald leaf that I had caught
Bore autumn's brown and yellow stain.

Cold Spring

Now the cold spring soaks with rain the dead grass,
And the grass grows green, but there is no sun.
The lilac buds wait for the sun and curl
Close to the wet bark of the throbbing branch.
Always the first green of the spring is cold,
And long after, when the sun comes, the green
Of leaves is cold. We had thought that in this land
Life and death would be things apart, would cry
Aloud to us with different voices;
We had thought that birth and the giving-up
Of breath would be two seasons of the world;
We had not thought to find the new grass
Cold in April, but the spring is a time
Of coldness even after the sun comes.
Somewhere in the recesses of the mind,
Unclouded by derision, there is a faith
In the two seasons of the world, in life
And death that do not walk together
In the mist. All the pain in the scent
Of lilacs, in the cold rain on the cheek,
Pricks with the edge of this remembered faith,
Which haunts the land of grasses and lilacs,
And cries aloud with many faint voices.
We do not hear these whispering voices,
Not even their echoes in the greening wood.

The Snake

Watching the terrible lithe loveliness
Of the snake rise in a gleaming arc of power straight
To the white unsuspecting flesh, I feel a shuddering orgasm
>of distress

Through the placid afternoon. Until the lightning-lifted
>head,
Beautiful and murderous, struck, fell limp from the body of
>desire,
Leaving it crumpled in the grass, I would not have said

Nature could be so futilely beautiful, could let
Spring from itself such silver-soaring strength and grace,
Taking in pure sleeping tenderness itself as target.

Ask Not of Me

Say not my eyes are a return;
Though I have been in many lands,
Volcanic peaks of time still burn
And throw a flame upon my hands.

Say not my voice is music's mood
When music accents song alone.
Though I have crossed heart's longitude,
The latitude remains unknown.

And I from realms of living dead
Still search the auguries of skies,
Withhold my word, and ask instead
A shining landmark from your eyes.

Say not my face and voice are deep
With having conquered time and death;
Too many leagues of life are sleep,
Too few are fire within our breath.

Ask not of me deliberate grace,
Peace from heart's regions I passed through;
I come a wanderer in this place,
And ask the tranquil road of you.

Night Quest

Past all acerbities of sun
                        the moon descends
In a shuttle of easy wind, weaving light liquescent.
Here evening is unhusked of gold and ends. . . .
   Calm argosy of day moves in this crescent.

Our courage stacked against disaster
                                     like sheaves mortised
With gold in morning has built no answer. Memory is lunar
                                               again,
Unwinding the skein of all that we have been. . . .
   Silence is the only alembic of our pain.

Is love then
              the answer or the armor?
All we can do is girdle the desperate day within our breath,
Ask no questions of the moon that floats its corolla there,
Thatching a remote unknowing world with sleep and death.

Voyage

Is there a strong brain-lurch toward death,
A quick heart-twist like the ship's plunge
In wild seas? O brothers, what is breath
But the body's reeling, a lunge

Through cloud-banked narrows of the day,
Across tympanic shoals of hate?
So yet the boisterous blood squalls say
That rare and blue-girt islands wait

Beyond the samite sheet of rain;
O take wind's push into your core
Arterial surge! We go amain
Turning the destined, wave-tossed oar

Toward death's island citadel.
Heart's careening is heaven-deep;
Breath is a sail that steers us well
Into the morning waves of sleep.

The Curtain of Rain

There is rain upon the roof and the dark
Colors of night are in the room. The faces
Of the listeners are pale in the darkness.
They listen to the rain as did their mothers,
They sit in the dark as did their fathers.
Sound of rain has been centuries long
Soft to the hearers. Always they have listened
For discord in the rainfall that would shatter
The monotone of time, that would break
The extended harmony of nature;
For the tirelessness of rain is tiring
To the hearer. A discord in its falling
Would be freedom to the senses. But the rain
Falls upon the snow and the green of spring,
Not in torrents, not in gushes, but dropping
Just as time falls, one moment on the other,
Lulling the senses, turning the brain
In rutted circles. Now in the darkness
The past sits with the present hearing the rain.
Drawn are the faces with awaiting the hearer
Who shall detect the discord, recapture
The freedom that long ages have deadened,
Who shall tear the curtain of rain into light.

Love Song

O come to me here at the edge
Of the world where the tufted sea
Beats like a bell tone on the ledge
Of the end of things, the end of me.

Does the land still sprout buds of death
Inland on the sensual bed?
I believe that the world's pure breath
Will stir the rose among the dead.

You have clung in the fold of man,
Sheep-like man, learned the body's route
And aped the passions of the clan;
You have fondled the human brute.

Beyond the limits of the flesh
I wait for you. Here at the world's rim
I salute the soul, tear the mesh
Of body, hail the seraphim.

This is the coast of repentance,
I wait for you. This is the citadel
Within man, beyond his sentence;
I wait where the sea beats like a bell.

Target Light

The light whereby I live my life
Bursts from the bulb of central thought.
The bed, the chair, the plate and knife
Lean rough and hard against the taut
Bright circle of the active brain.
The bladed smile, the hammering eyes
Strike at the source that lights my pain,
That burns against congealing lies.
And shadow ever stippling in
Hurls furious bludgeons of the night.
I hear within my room the din
Of blows upon the target light.
Yet so constant in this guarded place
Is crystal burning of the mind
That passions of another face
Can never keep its force confined.
And fear cannot usurp my chair
In a world close-shuttered and cold.
Against the dark the light is there;
The filaments of faith will hold.

The Hurt Look of Evil

It is a tawny afternoon: the field
Smothered in its own lushness, and I, awaiting
The least display of strength that will not yield

To the death-swoon of the dun-colored day, see a boy
Leap from the wood suddenly in a flawless reach of force,
Naked from darkness to clothe himself in joy.

The pure athletic angle of his body flung against dense skies
Crumples into a limp fold of flesh upon the grass.
Quivering: pathetic: with the hurt look of evil in his eyes,

He falls as the jackknife moment of power closes in light,
Leaving the inert meaningless instrument of his body
Beyond memory of desire: the spirit sheathed in night.

The Tree Stands Tenser

The tree stands tenser now,
   caught in an amber light.
The crackling burnished bough
   leans to the sword of night.
The malleable leaves are thrust
   under the sledge of wind;
With every hammering gust
   the foliage is thinned.
By weather are we taught
   the legend of the leaf:
The secret mind's green thought,
   bright cusps of our belief,
Sprung from an early bud,
   are shaped by seasons' pound;
The year's deciduous thud
   hurls them on glinting ground.
Our fortitude beat thin
   as leaves of tenuous gold
Seeks hardness deep within
   against the spear of cold.
We scan our inner world
   of mind galled bare and clean
To find a leaf unfurled
   with veins of crystal green.

The Truce

Listen: the world is here.
Yes: even past these walls the wind
Turns through channels of the ear.
All silences rescind
The threat of solitude.
Yes: past these walls the world
Knocks at the guarded inner door.
The cautious dissembling feud
I kept with time and space is held no more.
So on my shuttered senses light is hurled,
And from the corners of the darkened room
Rise the chair, the bed: all that leaping light uncovers.
Reason moves like a fresh-bound broom
Across the carpet of my fear.
The smothered distant mind discovers
The world is near!

Blind Would Be the Spirit

I have come early
                to hear the white psalm of the sea.
From the city's hysteria: its tarnished pathos. I shall stay
                                                                  late,
Breathing the day slowly: letting the hours like waves of
                                                                  purity

Enisle the mind
                a little while . . .
                                  I shall listen
To the heart's smooth saraband of blood: the demulcent
                                                                   wind:
The clear cry of children as they run from the water
                                                                  glistening.

Purer than any prayer
                    is the clean awe I feel
When girls and boys: bronzed: elate: limbs socketed with
                                                                life's ease
Pass by—given to the sun. Here nothing conceals

The body stripped to its truth. Blind would be the spirit
That would not walk naked with the animal
                                            clean and beautiful.
The mind, once scornful of the body,
                              is glad to be near it.

I have come early
                from the city: war: disaster.
                                              I shall stay late,

Clothing the spirit with cleanliness. Reaching by train at
                                                          night
The loud terminal of confusion where men and women wait,
Wearing tired frustrations over the body's light.

Nocturne

Close at the edge of night,
Under the hanging boughs,
I follow distant light
That twinkles from a house.
As long as light burns there,
Dilation of the mind
Holds the abundant air
Of day I leave behind.
Then past the lighted door
The leafy walk cuts far
Across the evening's floor
Magnetic to a star.
Wherever light wears thin
The leaf-thatch covers skies,
But brilliance held within
Gives vision to my eyes.
The vista of night's ease
Spreads wide as I see deep
Through portal of the trees
The miles of endless sleep.

THE BRIGHT PLAIN

Acknowledgments are due to the following magazines for permission to reprint poems: *Harper's, The Virginia Quarterly Review, The Yale Review, Poetry: A Magazine of Verse, The American Mercury, The North American Review, Voices, American Prefaces, The Southwest Review, The Lyric, The American Scholar, Fantasy, The Sewanee Review, Furioso, The Washington Post, The University Review* (Kansas City), and *Queen's Quarterly* (Canada).

THE

BRIGHT PLAIN

by

Charles Edward Eaton

CHAPEL HILL

The University of North Carolina Press

1942

COPYRIGHT, 1942, BY
THE UNIVERSITY OF NORTH CAROLINA PRESS

Contents

PART I
THE BRIGHT PLAIN

The Bright Plain	15
Spring Song	16
Green Regions	17
High Noon	18
Afternoon in Summer	19
Inlet	20
Stand Here: Near Me	21
Evening Equipoise	22
Tempo of the Night	23
Night Song	25
The Body's Dawn	26
Distant Victory	27

PART II
LANDSCAPE OF THE MIND

Landscape of the Mind	31
Cold Spring	32
The Snake	33
Ask Not of Me	34
Night Quest	35
Voyage	36
The Curtain of Rain	37
Love Song	38

Target Light	39
The Hurt Look of Evil	40
The Tree Stands Tenser	41
The Truce	42
Blind Would Be the Spirit	43
Nocturne	45

PART III

NIGHT TAKES THE CITY

Night Takes the City	49
Lost in Limbo	50
The Hunted	51
The Purchase	52
Declaration of the Snow	53
To Pedestrians of a Foreign Land	54
Other-Faces	55
Night Walk	56
Fountain	57
New Year	58
Street Scene	59
Beer Parlor	60
Equal Pace	61
Affirmation of the Evening	62

PART IV

SUMMIT AIR

Dark Summer	65
Talisman	66

Memory	67
Girls in White	68
Burning Leaves	69
A Ritual in Time of Death	70
The Purest Fact	72
A Play Called Eternity	73
Summit Air	74
These Are the Things of Youth	75
Vernal City	76
Summer Night	77
What Is the Earth Compounded of	78

PART V

DAWN FLIGHT

A Letter to a Young American	83
Air Raid	84
The Land Is Made of Light	85
Matinal	86
The Disparate Man	87
Old House	88
Pivot Place	89
Dawn Flight	90
Sheen of My Sensation	91
Light in Time Only	92

To

MY MOTHER AND FATHER

PART I

THE BRIGHT PLAIN

PART IV

SUMMIT AIR

Dark Summer

Slowly, as leaves glaze darker with the sun,
A sensual shadow moves across the mind.
Watching day die from the leaf veins in one
Twilight moment of deepening green, I find
Air shuddering over the placid house
With a thickening and drawing near of light;
Voluptuous the ease of hanging boughs
Strokes our listening love with fingers of the night.

Your face whose morning poise was bland with spring
Is a maze of shadow wind-sprung from the air.
You sit in a slowly narrowing ring
Of light's long fading on your evening hair,
Until through shattered windows of light worn thin,
The branches of desire bring summer dark within.

Talisman

There were your dark voice and my dark mind,
The taut caul of our hearts caulked tight.
There was the shadow-stippling wind
That hurled the needle of the night.

Rich morning blown past all belief
In the wind's seraphic rise
Swiftly dropped night's ebony leaf
Like augury before our eyes.

And all we tasted was the dark,
Deep mordant dust was on your hand.
The south star withered in its arc,
The moon, cloud-husked, was moored to land.

But suddenly I lanced my thought
For latent light I knew was there;
And when you turned and spoke we sought
The slow awakening of the air.

Racing our fingers through wide space,
We felt ascension of our breath;
The talisman of touch gave grace
To lips confounding night's sure death.

Memory

I remember a word: a face: a tear—
Brief play of light in deep eclipse of sense.
For here upon the carpets of my fear
The rooms of mind are darkened and immense.
Your amber shadow at the sunlit door:
Your hand against the curtain of the sun
Are lost in a haze upon the floor,
Littered with strands of a day unspun. . . .

I remember the liberal house of ease
Where the world in a lull of time and space
Was three sunlit walls and a window of trees
Until the evening's shadow crossed your face.
I remember the rapid frantic noise
Of breath staccato at the edge of night.

I think the fingers of my mind learn poise
And touch the switches of all inner light—
I turn within the room to find the chair
You sat in: the sheen of morning on your head.
But memory sits foolish and misshapen there
And speaks a maze of words you never said.

Girls in White

O look: the girls in white
With coils of yellow hair!
Where did they sleep last night—
In what house: in whose care?

Look: they walk hand in hand
Under white parasols.
Can't we make them understand
A dog waits by the walls?

Who let them walk alone,
Their eyes still pure with sleep?
A bad boy with a stone
Will hold their beauty cheap.

Immaculate of gear
They breathe the air of peace,
Remote from grief and fear
Since no one spoke of these.

Someone should stop them now
Before the night comes on;
A stranger with somber brow
Waits beyond the lawn.

Burning Leaves

Last night the southwest wind shook through the trees
And sheared them of golden leaves. The gutters
Are choked, and all the garden is covered
With golden drifts. I should like to have seen
Them falling one leaf on the other slowly
Until a wind-swell brought them down in torrents.
Destruction, in season, can be beautiful.
It was time for the leaves to be falling;
There would have been pleasure in watching them.
Tomorrow I shall be burning the leaf drifts.
It would be worse to leave them in the garden
To rot and blacken in the rain and snow.
Fire is the purest and most beautiful
Destroyer in nature. The leaves will have
A clean, quick death, and death in its going
Can be beautiful. I shall be glad to see
The skeletons of trees shake down their last
Leaves into the withering bright fire of bronze.
The crackle of burning leaves is a sharp
And poignant music, and blue smoke in my
Nostrils has the sweetest scent of autumn.
The destruction will be beautiful
In going until the fire has seared
Color from the leaf veins and the embers
Lie dead among the stones. The signs of burning
Are not lovely, and afterwards I shall
Wish I had left the leaves in the garden.
The fire stains will stay on stone and ground
All winter until spring comes to undo destruction.

A Ritual in Time of Death

Now a moving of brown hands,
Now a coughing against the wind. . . .
We have watched the gathering of fruit from the lands,
We have seen the lean-armed girls bind
Up the wheat. The ritual is slow,
Without sacrifice of blood, without fire.
Across the field there is a steady river-flow
Of stained, deliberate feet that never tire.
Has God gone merciless with dread?
Does the earth run out in a stream of juice?
Does youth taste rancid and are we fed
On dung the stallions, winter-shy, produce?
The hunter sounds his horn,
Death-loving, mutinous against the women's slow precision,
Golden-timbred among the corn.
The women spit roundly in derision,
Saying: Our feet are slower than earth's way.
We shall not die, we shall not hear the horn song;
We say fearlessly on this dying day
Earth does not control our hand, our heart, our tongue.
We do not cross ourselves at mass;
We make ritual in the field
Though bleeding swans, south-haunted, pass.
O Lord, we shall not yield,
O merciless God, we too are stone
Grown beautiful and flowering within,
Having taken the green within us. O limber our bone,
Willow-fresh our heart and free from the sin
Of death. O lovely and inner-clean
Are we! Look only beyond the body's citadel;

Brown our arms and hair but green
Is the spirit's depth, though hidden well.
Now are slow brown hands a subterfuge, the wisest lie—
Brave, stately ritual in time of death.
Tramping, O Lord, we breathe white steam against the sky
And guard the inner greenness of our breath.

O Lord, look inward. The ritual moves in time of death.

The Purest Fact

It is good to get there and find we know
the place, and find we knew it all along.
The heart's right knowledge: purest: happens so—
spun from its own spool: stretched like silken song
from its own light toward other brightness there;
The arch of thought in clear ultimate line:
simple: essential: exact: alone: and rare
joins with perfection functioned-smooth and shining.
It is good to walk in wide rooms of the mind
and stretch our arms toward walls we hope are near,
racing our hands through all the space we find
till solid touch: surest: makes time halt here—
poise in these copious rooms: the purest fact!

A Play Called Eternity

You don't have to joke. You don't have to be clever.
With that easy surface smile saying: too-smart-for-life-to-
    touch.
I can see a shining quick through your eyes
When you think no one's looking. A little quiver
And soft tremble of the mouth. Not much
To go on. But caught off-guard, you look right through
    your surprise,
And I can see you loving what's pure in me.
Suddenly in the street: seeing me clean.
Standing there without the wisecrack ways: gentle: all in
    light,
As though we were in a play called Eternity.
Light. Soft light. No one else coming in on the scene. . . .
Let's get moving. Your chum's calling. I feel inside like
    night,
And you're looking toward last week. Your eyes tired and
    late.
I want to take you home before dark to my place.
You can lie in my bed on a dream of tomorrow. I'll wait
Beside you . . . don't laugh . . . watching all night for
    morning on your face.

Summit Air

The streets of cities lead up hill
To sites of summit air where light
Attracts, elate, the men who will
Not build on lower levels of the night.

Magnetic to all height, they walk
From suburbs of chaotic sleep;
Metallic timbre of quickened talk
Diminishes as hills grow steep.

With valid will raised vertical,
Pedestrians cannot deny
The active impulse integral
To deep dimensions of the sky.

Though darkness has made disparate
What self had structurally defined,
They know pure altitudes await
The morning blueprints of the mind.

These Are the Things of Youth

These are the things of youth I remember—
The bright-imaged see-all-hear-all of quick,
Young senses, the tread of swift, muscled feet
Upon the walk, clear eyes reflecting
Pure sunlight, the rough tingling of blood
In the whole delightful, free-swinging,
Muscle-strung body. A man must be free in youth
With freedom that walks not lonely on the earth;
A man must be brother to all things living
And changing, the sprouting of the acorn,
The quick-paced, sensitive growing of his comrades—
This is the freedom youth promises, extends,
Impregnates in the bone marrow. The straight look,
The quick action, the mind not yet turned upon itself,
Not ferreting the heart with sneaking suspicion—
These are the things of youth I remember.
Not like old age, oblique, defeated, wearing
Its dignity in dress clothes, measuring the action
By the profit, fingering all ideals
Like counterfeit coins, breathing Wall Street's
Tomblike air—this is not the way
The young walk. They cast a straight shadow,
Not going on all fours, nor turning the claw
When the direct hit fails. Not hedged in, not broken!
These are the things of youth I remember.

Vernal City

Past the margins of greening lawn
Where leaves of lurching trees hang down,
We climb penumbral walks of dawn
To see if spring is in the town.

The country green we leave behind,
The foot-ease of the thawing field,
Fade from the morning urban mind
That seeks what green the town can yield.

The first to reach the silent square
Find pavements barren of all trees,
But after crowds have gathered there,
The day unfolds in vocal ease.

When narrow walks bring men together,
They read in eyes sufficient reason
To forecast clemencies of weather
And prophesy a change of season.

Against warm walls old men who lean,
Listening to the people talk,
Wait to hear the tone of green
In words of boys along the walk.

The fallow city finds a poise
Our quickened senses cannot lose;
Where bodies blend in vernal noise
We walk full pace in elastic shoes.

Summer Night

Looking tenderly through the crowded street,
I see too many people who-might-have-been,
Looking for someone to love them for what they never were.
An old coquette I meet
Smiles crookedly from depths behind her eyes, hoping I
                                                                    have seen
A white bright look beneath the cracked mask men call Her.
She stands a long time waiting for me to speak,
Hoping I'll say something simple and pure.
Under the streetlight trembling . . . a little afraid of the
                                                                      hard beams
That wilt the cheap rose of her sweaty cheek:
Still wanting to look demure
In her dirty green dress hung with a frayed fringe of old
                                                                      dreams.
I feel a shining in my hand,
And reach through the warm darkness toward what she is
                                                                      inside.
A long terror of human touch will not let her understand.
She shrinks suddenly: her eyes fill and look wide
Deep and dark out of the night,
Fearing my face: thinking my eyes see only out of the
                                                                      body's sight.

What Is the Earth Compounded of

What is the earth compounded of—
                         its own running away?
We walk upon a land sodded with morning and evening,
Trampling the green fire of approaching day.

There were stallions leaping, air tumultous with birds,
Tremendous assurance of life in the bursting shell of sun
Long before we were here . . . before we spoke these
                                       words:

Before this latest rapture of the blood
                         which is you . . . which is I,
There were millenniums of migrant mortal purposes
Pillowed on stone: laid prostrate under the blue cape of sky.

We walk upon our breath
                  that ripened long ago,
That still ripens and will ripen until the world's end.
We walk upon the fallen lives, the slow

Insistent plain whose subterranean depths are deep
With the respirations of eternity
Which time has thatched with silence and with sleep.

The moment of passion, the moment of poetry, of pity
Is the crust
        of this dust:
               is the mingled fragrance
That calms the specious pride of this wide city.

What is the earth compounded of?
                    . . . fallen, fallen . . .
We walk upon them fallen—hate, desire, and fear—
Bruising the calyx of creation as we walk,
                              while we spread
The petals of our breath. Let there be honor here.

PART V
DAWN FLIGHT

A Letter to a Young American

                    This is an American morning.
Sky is clear, and the sweet air tastes like melon;
The horizon is strung with racing birds,
Sun is a benediction upon the lands,
And breath is a prayer for a long, mild day.
                    Somewhere you wake in exile.
O my young friend, in resolute exile
In this very land! Last night you drew the blinds
And mortised your heart securely and slept,
Having put the door key by your pillow
As if you did not trust your countrymen.
Now you wake in a foreign port as you
Have done on other mornings, not knowing
How the voyage ended there, and not caring
When the next ship turns toward home, the green port.
                    I wrote you years ago
The real expatriate often stays at home.
Not an outer but an inner landscape
Is the love of land. The clear native word
Is babble to him who listens without love.
(Love simplifies all lexicons and grammars,
All language jagged in the mind.) You see
The land as one whose heart has suffered frostbite.
Love is like spring, and you have need of it
To change the season. I send you this letter
To bring you home into your native weather.
                    This is an American morning.
Do not forget the dark woods are greening.
My valediction, as you homeward turn,
Is, "Anchor and rest where the long voyage ends."
Postscript: My prayer will be answered: the day mild.

Air Raid

When the bombs have fallen
    upon the house of mind,
We rush upon the lawn
    through missile shards to find
Whatever held the house
    in lines distinct and pure
Lies under splintered boughs
    in debris of contour.
Where structure of desire
    suffers accurate hit
Solid walls of fire
    wither to rubbish pit.
But under exploded form
    of rubble and cinders,
Incapable of harm
    lie all of thought's members.
Unscathed by caustic flame
    lie the unbroken will:
The spirit we reclaim,
    denuded of all evil.

The Land Is Made of Light

I race against the clouds that take the hill:
Clouds over trees dripping light on my lawn.
When I look back the fountain's flare is still
A geyser of gold, jet-flawed as dark comes on.
Plunging from sudden clouds that taxi down
Like huge cosmic bombers freighted with night
A wind-release of darkness strikes the town,
And bombs of shadow hit the towers of light.

But I cannot run fast enough, nor shout
To men and women clothed in smooth-drawn sun:
"Run inside with light! Into the black-out
With brilliance before the air raid has begun!"
I put on darkness like a winter coat:
Acquaint my eyes with avenues of care.
There is not a bright vowel in my throat
After the black betrayal of the air.

I watch the children huddled in the park
Hiding their fear till the dense sky is stirred
By sun's last trajectory through the dark
Rising and lapsing on wings of a bird.
As sudden light moves in the pure-leaved trees,
Men open the portals of sun at every door.
The city rests on architraves of evening ease—
I know the land is made of light once more.

Matinal

From the somnolent city
    shored with frustrate dreams,
From precincts of self-pity
    razed by rocket flames,
The crowd with morning eyes—
    girls with glinting hair,
Well-knit boys trim of size—
    claim new ordinance of air.
Revoking sleep and death,
    charter of disaster,
They purge from wards of faith
    the demagogic master.
Ben's wisdom: Bert's aplomb:
    and the active love of Ann
Conceive millennium
    of integrated man.
The day incites the young
    to illusions of green trees
That lift themselves among
    cities of flawless ease.

The Disparate Man

The disparate man morning and night
    watches his neighbors' eyes—
John and Frank: the sullen and glad:
    the stupid and the wise.

They are not strangers to him:
    in glimpses of their smiles
Flash photographs of self
    that lie in memory's files.

The lavish introductions of the day
    teach arrogance to know
How variously to man
    the mind is apropos.

Duplicate feature: coincident thought:
    contingencies coerce
The disparate man to see himself
    composite with the universe.

Old House

The dead speak in this ancient house:
Whispering, whispering what they left unsaid.
Out on the lawn, through darkening boughs,
They breathe their shade around my head.

Their faces bloom from senses stirred
By rose nostalgia of the lawn;
I hear their faint wistaria word
Out of memory I have come upon.

They speak, saying: your hands are lent:
Eyes borrowed from us. Let us speak
Through the live mouth. Never is spent
Old blood running in the young cheek.

They cough in my blood, racking sleep—
Whispering: we are the dead you inherit.
Walking through all your dreams we keep
A lease upon the mortgaged spirit.

But when day breaks white the look I wear
Is more than father's eyes, grandpa's brow;
I walk in my self down the old stair,
Saying: No one but me lives here now.

Pivot Place

To be godlike is suddenly wise,
To look down purely from an evening hill
Of passionless air. Where summit cannot rise
To higher altitude, I hold no feud with will.
Men are walking below in the twilight;
Remote: clothed like heroes in sun's last strength;
Proud movers across the mosaic night,
They haze into the deepening shade at length.

It is good to be godlike, to be far
In order to be near. Each hero face
Stipples the night of the world like a star:
Love finds its axis in this pivot place,
And sky is suddenly vault of my brain,
Waiting for light over loved land again.

Dawn Flight

Close by valor's hangar
He sees blue fusilage,
Dim in propeller's haze.
Where shoals of fog spread far,
Gray shapes of a mirage
Haunt his compass gaze.

No instruments declare
When darkness will unwind
The coil of mist and cloud;
Yet in constricted air
He flies the distance blind
Between free sky and ground.

We watch him scale the night
From airdromes of concern.
Gauging the shadows close,
He plumbs a rift of light:
From darkness yet to learn
The altitude of cosmos.

Sheen of My Sensation

From sheen of my sensation flows the dawn.
Caught in the bombed suburbs shuddering with night,
I see how sensual is time, moving on
From slow darkness to a long reach of light.
There was a city of desire that rose
On a pure morning in another world;
We never thought air would tarnish and close,
Blighting the flower of dawn that light unfurled.

The darkness where all time is sensual
Brings black cities: dark eyes: night over mind.
Yet fingers of our sensitive love recall
The dazzling walls of day and still can find
A wide warm width flowing from night where much
Fell dead and cold beyond the sheen of touch.

Light in Time Only

We can never put out the light
In the look of love. Not like morning-shine or noon-sheen:
The glimmering glaze of trees: the river's bright loop of
                                                    gold:
The dazzling deliquescence of falling water seen
Bright-once-only: cascaded a long depth down toward night.
These have light-in-time-only. What sky can hold
Twice over the same dapple of dawn?
I ask, knowing that all our symbols for love: life of the mind
Are caught from the lilt of the world drawn
Over the dam of desire. No wonder we find
Surface instead of source: naming thing-ness with a
                                        waterflow of word:
Leaving light-only-of-love in the body's depth: limitless and
                                                    unstirred.

www.ingramcontent.com/pod-product-compliance
Lightning Source LLC
Chambersburg PA
CBHW020753230426
43665CB00009B/584